SPRINTS, HURDLES, AND OTHER TRACK EVENTS
by Jason Page

CONTENTS

Crabtree Publishing Company
www.crabtreebooks.com

Editor: Robert Walker
Proofreader: Mike Hodge
Acknowledgements: We would like to thank Ian Hodge, Richard Mead and Elizabeth Wiggans for their assistance.
Cartoons by: John Alston

Picture Credits: t = top, b = bottom, l = left, r = right, OFC = outside front cover, OBC = outside back cover, IFC =front cover
All images courtesy of Allsport, except for Lutz Bongarts/ Bongarts/ Getty Images: 30. Matthew Fearn/ PA Archive/ PA Photos: 16/17. Gouhier- Kempinaire/ Cameleon/ ABACA/ PA Photos: 12/13c. Dave and Les Jacobs/ Getty Images: OFC. Glyn Kirk/ Action Plus: 18/19c. Sipa Press/ Rex Features: 27br.
Picture research by Image Select

Library and Archives Canada Cataloguing in Publication

Page, Jason.
  Sprints, hurdles, and other track events / Jason Page.

(The Olympic sports)
Includes index.
ISBN 978-0-7787-4018-6 (bound).--ISBN 978-0-7787-4035-3 (pbk.)

  1. Track and field--Juvenile literature. 2. Olympics--Juvenile literature. I. Title. II. Series: Page, Jason. Olympic sports.

GV1060.55.P34 2008   j796.42   C2008-900976-2

Library of Congress Cataloging-in-Publication Data

Page, Jason.
  Sprints, hurdles, and other track events / Jason Page.
    p. cm. -- (The Olympic sports)
  Includes index.
  ISBN-13: 978-0-7787-4018-6 (rlb)
  ISBN-10: 0-7787-4018-8 (rlb)
  ISBN-13: 978-0-7787-4035-3 (pb)
  ISBN-10: 0-7787-4035-8 (pb)
  1. Track and field--Juvenile literature. 2. Olympics--Juvenile literature. I. Title. II. Series.

GV1060.55.P34 2008
796.42--dc22
                                              2008004954

Crabtree Publishing Company
www.crabtreebooks.com   1-800-387-7650

Published in Canada
Crabtree Publishing
616 Welland Ave.
St. Catharines, Ontario
L2M 5V6

Published in the United States
Crabtree Publishing
PMB16A
350 Fifth Ave., Suite 3308
New York, NY 10118

TRACK EVENTS

There are two sorts of athletic events: field events (throwing or jumping), and track events (races). In the Olympic Games, there are 30 different track events, and each one is covered in this book...

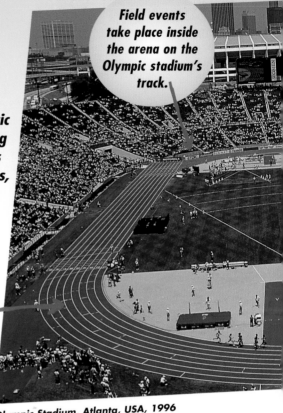

Field events take place inside the arena on the Olympic stadium's track.

In short-sprint races, athletes must stay inside their own lane, but in middle- and long-distance events, they can cross over into other lanes.

Olympic Stadium, Atlanta, USA, 1996

SUPER STATS

All of the track events at the 2008 Olympic Games start and finish inside Beijing's National Stadium, which is commonly called the "Bird's Nest." The stadium can seat 91,000 spectators and could fit four jumbo jets inside it!!

ANCIENT ORIGINS

The first records of the ancient Olympic Games date from 776 BCE. At this time, just one competition was included. This was a track event known as the "stadion," a 210 yard (192m) running race. The first recorded winner (and the first recorded Olympic champion) was a cook named Koroibos.

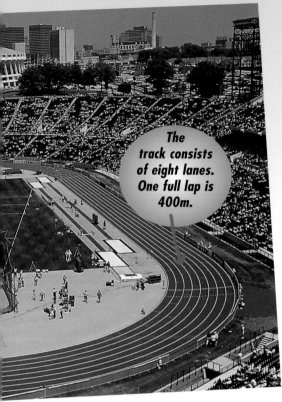

The track consists of eight lanes. One full lap is 400m.

BRAVO PAAVO!

One of the greatest Olympic track athletes of all time was Paavo Nurmi (FIN) who won a total of 12 medals (nine gold and three silver) at the Games between 1920 and 1928. Nurmi competed in seven different middle- and long-distance events. Perhaps his most remarkable achievement was winning the 5000m race just 30 minutes after winning the 1,500m!

OLYMPICS FACT-FILE

The Olympic Games were first held in Olympia, in ancient Greece, around 3,000 years ago. They took place every four years until they were abolished in 393 CE.

A Frenchman called Pierre de Coubertin (1863–1937) revived the Games, and the first modern Olympics were held in Athens in 1896.

The modern Games have been held every four years since 1896, except in 1916, 1940, and 1944, due to war. Special 10th anniversary Games took place in 1906.

The symbol of the Olympic Games is five interlocking colored rings.

HOT STUFF

Wherever the Olympic Games go, the Olympic flame goes too! A burning torch will be carried all the way from Olympia in Greece, the site of the ancient Olympic Games. A relay team of 5000 runners will transport the flame across the world to reach Beijing for the opening ceremony.

mpic flame, ul, 1988

RUN FOR IT

One race with ancient origins is the marathon. This was inspired by the story of an ancient Greek messenger named Pheidippides, who ran 26 miles to bring news of the great Battle of Marathon. Unfortunately, after delivering his message, Pheidippides died of exhaustion!

Marion Jones (USA)

DISGRACED STAR

Marion Jones (USA) was a favorite going into the 2000 Sydney Games, and told the press she could win five gold medals. At the Games, Jones won three gold medals and two bronze medals, but was later disqualified. It was found she had been taking banned drugs to enhance her performance. She had to return all of the medals in October 2007.

DID YOU KNOW?

♫ Runners in the 100m hold their breath until the end of the race!

♫ In 1992, at the age of 32, Linford Christie (GBR) became the oldest person ever to win the 100m.

♫ The 1900 and 1904 Olympic Games included an even shorter sprint of just 60m.

Starting block

The starting blocks are fitted with pressure-sensitive pads. These can detect if an athlete starts moving before the starting pistol has been fired. Each athlete is allowed to make one false start — but a second offence means instant disqualification!

STARTING ORDERS

At the start of a sprint race, the official in charge shouts "On your marks!" When they hear this, the eight runners kneel down and place their feet in the starting blocks. The starter then shouts "Set!," at which the runners lift their hips, raise both their knees off the ground, and wait for the starting pistol to be fired.

MEN'S RECORDS – WORLD: Asafa Powell (JAM) – 9.74 sec. **OLYMPIC**: Donovan Bailey (CAN) 9.84 sec.

THE 100 METER

The shortest of the great sprint races, the 100m has been part of the modern Games ever since they began.

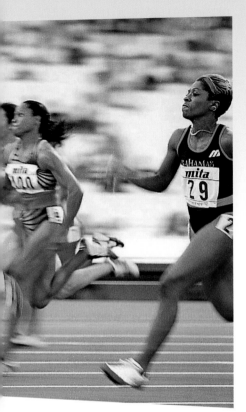

BE SURE TO DIP

Have a good look at the 100m sprinters in action. If you watch closely, you will notice how they thrust their chests out just before they cross the finish line. This is known as "dipping." It pushes their bodies forward and knocks a couple of hundredths of a second off of their time — which can mean the difference between winning gold and coming in second!

SCANDAL!

Sadly, a few Olympic athletes don't play by the rules. One of the worst cases of cheating occurred in the men's 100m final at the 1988 Olympics. Ben Johnson (CAN) was first to cross the finish line in a new world-record time. However, just three days later, he was stripped of both his medal and record when it was discovered that he had taken banned drugs to improve his performance.

ANIMAL OLYMPIANS

The fastest human athletes reach a top speed of around 25 MPH (40.2 KM/H) , but the cheetah can knocks the spots off that. This powerful big cat can sprint at up to 62 MPH (99.8 KM/H)!

THE 200 METER

The first half of this race is run on a bend in the track.
It requires a special sprinting skill to maintain a steady running rhythm while turning to the left!

HAVING A GOOD TIME

Michael Johnson's (USA) winning time of 19.32 seconds in the 200m at the 1996 Games not only won him the gold medal, but also set a new world record!

SUPER STATS

200 METER

I	JAMAICA
II	CANADA
II	ITALY
I	USSR
III ︲︲︲ ︲︲︲ ︲︲︲	USA

The finals of the Men's 200m have been held 24 times at the Olympics. The Soviet Union (USSR) and Jamaica have both won once. Canada and Italy have each had two victories. The other 18 gold medals have all been won by the USA.

STAGGERING AROUND

Both the 200m and 400m have "staggered" starts. This means instead of lining up together in a straight line (as they do in the 100m), the runners in the inside lanes start behind those in the outside lanes. This compensates for the curve in the track and ensures that each athlete runs exactly the same distance.

GOLDEN RECORD

Women competed in the 200m for the first time in 1948. The race was won by Fanny Blankers-Koen (NED) who also won the 100m, the 100m hurdles, and the 4x100m relay. Her total of four gold medals at one Games is a record for any female athlete!

starting pistol

GOOD SHOT

The pistol used to start the 200m races is fired next to a microphone. The microphone carries the sound to speakers placed behind each of the starting blocks. This ensures that all the athletes hear the bang at exactly the same time. Without these speakers, the runner closest to the gun would hear it a fraction of a second before the others and get a head start.

DID YOU KNOW?

No man has ever won the 200m twice!

In 1904, the men's 200m was won by Archie Hahn (USA) after all the other runners had been given a 2m handicap for false starts!

In the 1932 final, one of the lanes used was 1.5m longer than all the others!

Eric Liddell (GBR)

GOD SPEED

Eric Liddell (GBR) won the 400m in 1924 — despite the fact that he had spent months training for the 100m instead! Liddell was a devout Christian and refused to run in the 100m because the final was on a Sunday, which the Bible says should be a day of rest. Remarkably, Liddell not only came in first in the 400m, he also broke the world record.

DID YOU KNOW?

All races over 110m (120 yards) must be run counter-clockwise!

In 1984, Valerie Brisco-Hooks (USA) became the first person in Olympic history to win both the 200m and the 400m at the same Games!

A film called Chariots of Fire was based on Eric Liddell's story.

WORLD CHAMP

Marie José Pérec (FRA) won the women's 200m at the 1992 and 1996 Olympics but could not win for a third time in 2000. She lost to Australian runner Cathy Freeman, much to the delight of the host nation. However, Marie José Pérec still holds the Olympic record.

THE 400 METER

This is the longest of the sprint races — and the toughest! Competitors run flat-out all the way around the Olympic running track.

NO COMPETITION

In 1908, the men's 400m was won by Wyndham Halswelle (GBR). It was the easiest victory in Olympic history — because Halswelle was the only person in the race! He ran solo in a re-run after the original winner was disqualified and the other two finalists withdrew in protest.

LIGHT WORK

Originally, a thin piece of thread or tape was stretched across the finishing line. Nowadays, this has been replaced by an invisible beam of light. A sensor detects the moment that the light is broken by one of the runners crossing the line and automatically records the winning time.

Marie José Pérec (FRA)

ANIMAL OLYMPIANS

Modern Olympic athletes fly around the 400m running track in under 50 seconds. But a duck could fly around much faster! Ducks are among the fastest flying birds, with a top speed of over 62 MPH (99.8 km/h). This means they would take just 14 seconds to fly 400m!

WOMEN'S RECORDS – WORLD: Marita Koch (GDR) – 47.60 sec. **OLYMPIC:** Marie José Pérec (FRA) – 48.25 sec.

THE 4X100 METER RELAY

This race is all about teamwork. The teams are made up of four runners who each run 100m.

TAKE THE TUBE

Modern relay runners carry a short hollow tube called a "baton". It's about 12 inches (30cm) long and weighs at least 1.7 ounces (50g) — that's about as heavy as a golf ball. If runners drop the baton during a race, they must pick it up again before continuing.

SUPER STATS

The women's world record in the 4x100m is just .59 seconds slower than four times the women's world record for the 100m!

The moment when one runner passes the baton to another is called a "changeover." Relay runners spend many hours practicing their changeovers to make them as smooth and fast as possible.

Practicing changeover

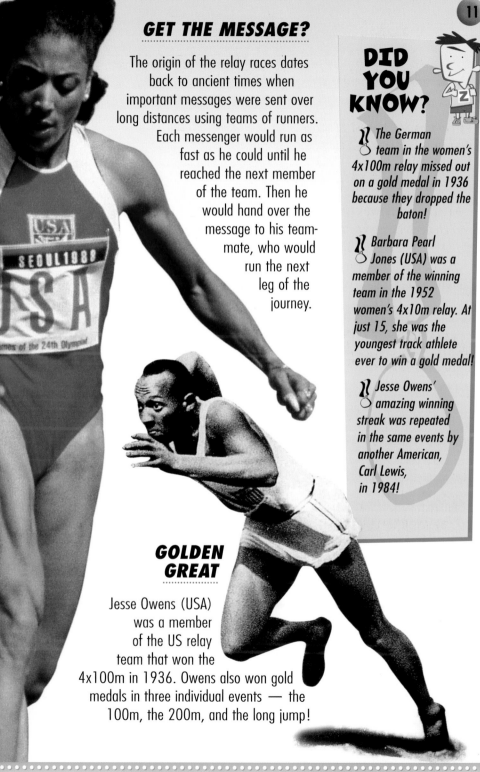

GET THE MESSAGE?

The origin of the relay races dates back to ancient times when important messages were sent over long distances using teams of runners. Each messenger would run as fast as he could until he reached the next member of the team. Then he would hand over the message to his team-mate, who would run the next leg of the journey.

DID YOU KNOW?

The German team in the women's 4x100m relay missed out on a gold medal in 1936 because they dropped the baton!

Barbara Pearl Jones (USA) was a member of the winning team in the 1952 women's 4x10m relay. At just 15, she was the youngest track athlete ever to win a gold medal!

Jesse Owens' amazing winning streak was repeated in the same events by another American, Carl Lewis, in 1984!

GOLDEN GREAT

Jesse Owens (USA) was a member of the US relay team that won the 4x100m in 1936. Owens also won gold medals in three individual events — the 100m, the 200m, and the long jump!

SUPER STARS & STRIPES

The men's 4x400m relay was held for the first time at the Olympics in 1912. It was won by the USA, which has dominated the event ever since. In fact, the US team has won 16 out of the 21 finals. This picture shows them celebrating their victory at Sydney in 2004.

USA men's 4x400m relay team

DID YOU KNOW?

)) In 1988, Olga Brzygina (URS) won gold medals in the women's 4x400m relay and the 400m, while her husband Viktor won a gold medal in the men's 4x10m!

)) The 4x400m relay is not run in lanes, so runners have to look behind them as they take the baton. Runners in the less chaotic 4x100m don't need to do this!

)) The part of the race run by each member of a relay team is called a "leg" – so you could say all relay runners have one leg!

BREAKING LANES

Unlike runners in the 4x100m relay, those in the 4x400m don't have to stay in their lanes. However, they must make sure that they don't get in each others' way — particularly in the changeover zone!

Relay changeover

THE 4X400 METER RELAY

This relay is four times longer than the other Olympic relay race — which makes it four times as tough!

FIRST AND LAST

The first relay race ever held at the modern Olympics was a medley relay which took place in 1908. Instead of all the athletes running the same distance, the first and second runners ran 200m, the third ran 400m and the last ran 800m (a total of 1,600m). The race was won by the USA, but was never held again.

ZONE LIMITS

Athletes must pass the baton to their teammates inside the changeover zone. This stretch of track is 20m long, and special markings show where it begins and ends. Competitors are allowed to start running before they have been handed the baton, but they mustn't pass beyond the end of the zone without it — if they do, their team will be disqualified!

Races have gotten faster and faster! The current men's world record is now more than 20 seconds faster than the winning time in the first ever Olympic 4x400m relay held in 1912.

THE 800 METER

This is the first of the two middle-distance races held at the Olympics. It's a test of stamina as well as speed.

GIRL POWER

The men's 800m has been held at every single Olympic Games. The women's event was introduced in 1928, but wasn't held again until 1960. This was because the men who organized the Olympics were worried that women weren't strong enough to run such a long race. However, female athletes have since proved them wrong — in fact, the women's 800m record is now 18 seconds faster than the winning time in the men's event of 1896!

RUNNING FLAT-OUT

The longer the race, the more exhausting it is for the runner. In the 1996 Games, Vebjorn Rodal (NOR) had used up all of his strength by the end of the men's 800m final, as the picture shows. Still, it was worth it — he won the gold medal and set a new Olympic record!

Vebjorn Rodal (NOR)

ANIMAL OLYMPIANS

The common flea can cover 13 inches (33cm) with a single jump. That's about 220 times the length of its own body. If humans could do the same, we would be able to complete the 800m with just two leaps!

MEN'S RECORDS – WORLD: Wilson Kipketer (DEN) – 1 min. 41.11 sec. **OLYMPIC**: Vebjorn Rodal (NOR) – 1 min. 42.58 sec.

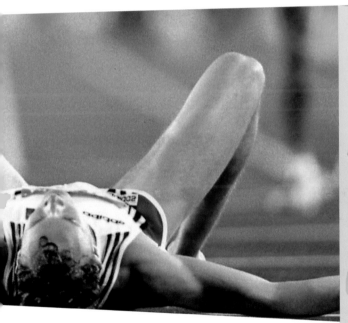

Racing tactics

BOXING MATCH

Tactics play a big part in winning a race. A runner who doesn't watch out can end up being "boxed in" — in other words, surrounded by a group of other runners and prevented from taking the lead. This is what has happened to the runner wearing number 151 in this picture.

DID YOU KNOW?

The 800m begins with a staggered start, but once the runners pass the first bend, they are allowed to disregard their lanes and move to the inside of the track.

In 1992, the gold and silver medalists in the 800m men's final were separated by only 4/100th of a second!

The 1928 women's 800m was won by 24-year-old Lina Radke-Batschauer (GER) — the first individual gold medal won by a German competitor at the Olympics!

ON THE BALL

At the 1992 Games, the gold medal in the women's 800m was won by Ellen Van Langen (NED). However, Van Langen began her sporting career not as an athlete but as a soccer player! Four years before her Olympic triumph, she was playing in the Dutch national women's team.

Kelly Holmes (GBR)

All athletes must wear a number on their clothing. This is used by race officials to identify them.

A runner's clothing needs to be light and flexible. Tight-fitting clothes make the athlete's body more streamlined and aerodynamic.

THE 1500 METER

The men's 1500m has been part of every Olympics since the modern Games began, but the women's event was not introduced until 1972.

DOING THE DOUBLE

So far, eight athletes have won both middle-distance races at the same Games. Kelly Holmes (GBR), pictured right, is the most recent. She took the gold in the 800m and the 1500m at Athens in 2004.

MEN'S RECORDS – WORLD: Hicham El Guerrouj (MAR) – 3 min. 26 sec. **OLYMPIC:** Noah Ngeny (KEN) 3 min. 32.07 sec.

Runners wear light-weight shoes with short spikes on the soles. The spikes help to grip the running track and stop the athlete from slipping.

Start of the 1500m

GETTING GOING

Unlike shorter races, the 1500m doesn't begin with a staggered start. Instead, runners form a curved line across the track and are allowed to break from their lanes as soon as the starting pistol is fired.

ANIMAL OLYMPIANS

The diplodocus was one of the longest dinosaurs that ever roamed Earth, but it wasn't nearly as long as the 1500m race! In fact, you would need more than 55 of these giant dinos placed nose-to-tail to reach from the start to the finish line.

WOMEN'S RECORDS – WORLD: Yunxia Qu (CHN) – 3 min. 50.46 sec. **OLYMPIC**: Paula Ivan (ROM) – 3 min. 53.96 sec.

SHORT-SPRINT HURDLES

The short-sprint hurdles race requires total concentration. The smallest mistake can lead to disaster — as athlete Gail Devers discovered!

SPOT THE DIFFERENCE

In all hurdle races there are 10 hurdles to jump. The difference is in the height of the hurdle and the length of the track. The men's short-sprint event is 110m long — that's 10m longer than the women's event. The men's hurdles are also slightly higher — 42 inches (106.7cm) compared to 33 inches (83.8cm).

GOING...

GOING...

GONE...

Gail Devers (USA)

FALLING AT THE FINAL HURDLE

In the 1992 Games, Gail Devers (USA) was in the lead during the final of the 100m hurdles when she hit the last hurdle with her foot. This mistake cost her the race. She lost her balance, stumbled and fell over the line in fifth place. Five days earlier, Devers had won the 100m sprint. Had she also won the hurdles, she would have become the first woman in Olympic history to take the gold in both events.

MEN'S RECORDS - WORLD: Liu Xiang (CHN) 12.88 sec. **OLYMPIC**: Liu Xiang (CHN) 12.91 sec.

Liu Xiang celebrates after winning the gold medal at the 2004 Athens Games. It was his country's first gold medal in athletics since the Atlanta Games eight years before.

Liu Xiang (CHN)

UP, UP, & AWAY!

As a hurdler leaps over a jump, the pushes his front leg straight out. His other leg follows, knee-first, and is kept bent, sweeping low and flat over the top of the hurdle. Hurdlers must spend hours practicing their jumping technique to ensure a perfectly smooth running rhythm.

DID YOU KNOW?

In both the men's and the women's short-sprint hurdles, athletes take three strides between each jump.

Hurdlers are allowed to knock the hurdles down, but if their feet pass by the sides of the hurdles below the height of the crossbar, they will be disqualified.

Until 1968, the women's short-sprint hurdles race was just 80m long.

WOMEN'S RECORDS – WORLD: Yordanka Donkova (BUL) – 12.21 sec. OLYMPIC: Joanna Hayes (USA) 12.37 sec.

THE ONE & ONLY

Only one athlete has ever won both the 400m and 400m hurdles. His name was Harry Hillman (USA), and he achieved this remarkable feat back in 1904. However, the hurdles used in Hillman's race were 6 inches (15cm) shorter than the hurdles used today.

MIGHTY MOSES

Edwin Moses (USA) won the men's 400m hurdles at the 1976 Olympics and set a new world record. The following year saw the beginning of a winning streak for him which lasted almost 10 years! He won every single one of his next 122 races, including another Olympic gold in 1984.

DID YOU KNOW?

The hurdles in the 400m are lower than the ones used in the short-sprint hurdles — 36 inches (91.4cm) high in the men's event, and 30 inches (76.2cm) high in the women's.

Hurdles are designed so that they will fall over when the crossbar is hit by a force of at least (7.9 pounds) 3.6 kg.

Edwin Moses would almost certainly have won another Olympic gold in 1980. However, US athletes refused to compete in the Games that year because of a political protest.

Edwin Moses (USA)

WARM-UP TECHNIQUE

All athletes have to warm up before they compete to help prevent injuries such as torn muscles. A good warm-up exercise for hurdlers is called "ground hurdling." This involves sitting down with one leg stretched out in front of you and the other bent around behind you, then bending forward as far as possible. Stretching a leg out along the top of a hurdle is also a good way to warm up!

THE 400 METER HURDLES

The hurdles are shorter in this race, but sprinting for 400m is a big part of the challenge!

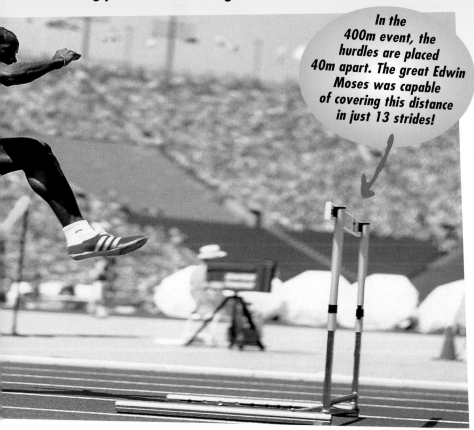

In the 400m event, the hurdles are placed 40m apart. The great Edwin Moses was capable of covering this distance in just 13 strides!

Tony Jarrett (GBR)

At 30 inches (76cm) high, the hurdles used in the women's 400m are about half as tall as you are. But even the shortest hurdles are a tall order if you have to jump over 10 of them in a row!

SUPER STATS

THE STEEPLECHASE

At 3000m long, with 28 hurdles and 7 water jumps to clear, the steeplechase is one intimidating race!

LEADING THE CHARGE

This picture shows Joseph Keter (KEN) lagging behind his countryman Moses Kiptanui in the 1996 Atlanta Games, but Keter then went on to win the race! Kenya has completely dominated this event — at the last six Olympics, Kenyan athletes have won six gold medals, five silver medals and two bronze medals!

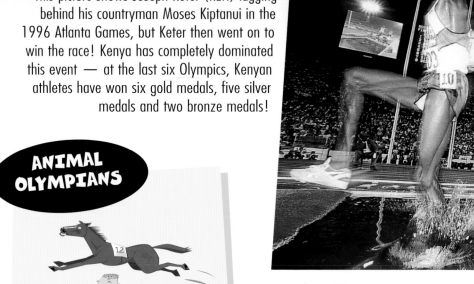

ANIMAL OLYMPIANS

The steeplechase is named after a type of horse race that involves jumping over hedges and ditches. If horses were to race against humans, they would gallop away with the gold. They can run twice as fast and can clear jumps two-and-a-half times higher than the steeplechase hurdles.

Unlike the other hurdles, these ones are sturdy and can't topple over.

MEN'S 110M
height: 42 inches
width: 4 feet

WOMEN'S 100M
height: 33 inches
width: 4 feet

MAKING A SPLASH

Competitors jump straight over the hurdles but when they come to the water jump, they step on the crossbar. Leaping from the top of the barrier enables them to jump farther and clear more of the water. However, it's impossible not to land with a splash, and everyone ends up with wet feet!

LANDING IN DEEP WATER

The bottom of the water trough is sloped so the water gets shallower the further you jump. The trough is deepest near the hurdle. The water here is 28 (71.1 cm)inches deep — if you stood in it, it would come up to your middle!

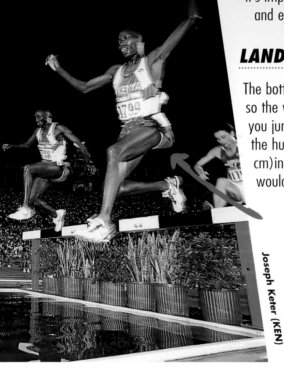

Joseph Keter (KEN)

DID YOU KNOW?

Only men take part in the steeplechase internationally. However, women compete in this sport at a national level in many countries.

To cover 3000m takes 7.5 laps of the running track. Each lap has four hurdles and one water jump.

In the 1932 Olympics, the winner of the steeplechase ran an extra lap by mistake!

HURDLING HEIGHTS

Steeplechase hurdles are the same height as the ones used in the men's 400m hurdles race. The hurdles are 13 feet (3.9m) wide — much wider than the hurdles used in other races. This is because all of the competitors go over the same jumps.

STEEPLECHASE
height: 36 inches
width: 13 feet

MEN'S 400M
height: 36 inches
width: 4 feet

WOMEN'S 400M
height: 30 inches
width: 4 feet

LONG WAIT

Women athletes had to wait until 1984 before they could take part in long-distance races at the Olympics. A 3000m race and women's marathon were finally introduced when the Games came to Los Angeles in 1984. Four years later, in Seoul, women were allowed to compete in the 10,000m for the first time. In 1996 the women's 3000m was replaced by the 5000m — which means, at long last, the women's and men's long-distance events are the same!

Junxia Wang (CHN)

DID YOU KNOW?

Nowadays, athletes are given their medals in a grand ceremony in front of the crowd, but when the modern Olympics first started, medals were sometimes sent out in the mail.

Athletes in middle- and long-distance races are not allowed to use starting blocks.

There used to be a 5000m team race. It was held only once, in 1900, when it was won by a team made up of British and Australian runners.

THE 5000 METER

When the going gets tough, the tough get going. And in the 5000m race, they've got a long way to go!

...ANG WINS

...e first woman to win an Olympic gold
...edal in the 5000m was Junxia Wang
...HN) at Atlanta in 1996. Her winning
...e at Atlanta was just a fraction of a
...ond under 15 minutes and set
...ew Olympic record. Wang's
...rd has since been
...ken twice.

IN TRAINING

Long-distance races test the athletes' fitness and stamina to the limits. Competitors have to spend countless hours training and run up to 93 miles (149.7 km) every week in order to stay in peak condition. That's the same as 375 laps of an Olympic running track!

FAMOUS FIVE

Five athletes have won both the 5000m and the 10,000m at the same Games. Vladimir Kuts (URS) achieved this remarkable double when the Olympics were held in Australia back in 1956.

ANIMAL OLYMPIANS

The pronghorn antelope is the long-distance running champion of the animal kingdom. It can maintain a steady speed of 35 MPH (56.3 KM/H) over a distance of 5,000m. No other animal can travel so far so fast!

Vladimir Kuts (URS)

THE 10,000 METER

This is the longest race that is held inside the Olympic stadium — athletes have to cover 25 laps of the track!

AFRICA UNITED

In 1992, athletes from South Africa were able to compete at the Olympic Games for the first time in 32 years! They had been banned until this time because of their government's apartheid policy, which kept black and white people apart. However, when this policy was ended, so was the ban. Elana Meyer (RSA) celebrated her country's return to the Games with a silver medal in the women's 10,000m, finishing six seconds behind Derartu Tulu (ETH).

ANIMAL OLYMPIANS

Traveling at top speed without taking any rests, it would take a garden snail more than eight days to finish the 10,000m!

Elana Meyer (RSA)

THINKING WITH YOUR FEET

Winning a long-distance race requires mental tactics, as well as physical stamina. Runners have to plan how they are going to use their energy reserves. Some try to surprise their opponents with a sudden burst of speed a whole lap before the end of the race, while others save all of their energy for the final sprint just before the finish.

DID YOU KNOW?

The current world record in the 10,000m is 5 minutes faster than the winning time in the 1912 Olympics!

Finland has won the men's 10,000m more times than any other country, with seven victories to its credit.

The 10,000m race takes more than 160 times longer to run than the 100m race!

SETTING THE PACE

World records in long-distance events are rarely broken at the Olympic Games. This is because all of the competitors are trying to win, so there's usually no one to act as a "pacemaker" — someone who leads the race at the beginning and sets a fast pace for the others to follow. Pacemakers help other athletes break records, but because they start out so quickly, they are usually exhausted before they reach the finish line.

WINNER'S SONG

At the 2004 Games Kenenisa Bekele (ETH) won the gold medal in 10,000m and the silver in the 5000m. Bekele also holds the world record in the 10,000m and even had a song written about him called *History is Made*.

Kenenisa Bekele (ETH)

WOMEN'S RECORDS – WORLD: Wang Junxia (CHN) – 29 mins. 31.78 sec. **OLYMPIC**: Derartu Tulu (ETH) – 30 mins. 17.49 sec.

A NICE BRISK WALK

Walking races are very long! The Women's event is 10km long. There are two men's events. One is the 20km and the other is the whopping 50km — that's longer than the marathon!

Women's 10km walk

DID YOU KNOW?

The 50km walk is the equivalent of 125 laps of the Olympic track.

There have been several other walking events in Olympic history — including a 1500m walk!

Walking races start and finish in the Olympic stadium, but most of the race takes place in the surrounding streets.

WIGGLE IT!

By swinging their hips from side to side, walkers can increase the length of their stride. This means they travel farther with each step — but it also means that they look quite silly!

Andrzej Chylinski (USA)

WALKING RACES

A walking race sounds easy enough, but there's a lot more to them than you probably think!

LEARNING TO WALK

In a walking race, the rule is that you must keep one foot on the ground at all times. In other words, you must not lift your back foot up until you've put your front foot down. Your back leg must also be straightened for a moment while your back foot is on the ground. Give it a try — it's not as easy as it sounds, especially if you're trying to walk quickly.

WARNING SIGNALS

Judges keep a close eye on the walkers. If a competitor is spotted breaking the rules, the judge will show a disc as a warning. If the competitor then commits a second offence, another disc will be raised signaling that he has been disqualified.

SUPER STATS

Medal-winning walkers achieve an average speed of more than 9 MPH (14.5 KM/H) — that's half as fast as a sprint champion, but twice as fast as an Olympic swimmer!

THE MARATHON

The marathon is a gruelling 42km run through the streets of the Olympic city. It's the ultimate test of stamina and determination!

BY ROYAL COMMAND

The first modern Olympic marathons were 40km long. However, when the Games came to London in 1908, the race was lengthened slightly to 42.195 km. This was because the British royal family wanted to watch the start of the race in front of Windsor Castle! This distance was then adopted as the official length of the Olympic marathon.

ANIMAL OLYMPIANS

When it comes to marathon journeys, the Caribou's annual trip across North America takes some beating. These large deer travel up to 25,000 miles (40,233.6 km) every year — the equivalent of almost 1,000 marathon races.

25 000mi

NOT FAIR!

Dorando Pietri (ITA) was the unluckiest marathon runner in Olympic history. At the Games in 1908, Pietri was leading the race as he entered the Olympic stadium. However, he collapsed from exhaustion four times on the final lap of the track. Eventually, two race officials helped him across the finish line. Although Pietri finished first, he was disqualified — because the judges said he had "used external support," which is against the rules!

GOING THE DISTANCE

Naoko Takahashi (JPN), pictured left, crosses the finish line during the women's Marathon final at the Sydney Olympic Games. Takahashi still holds the women's Olympic record for the event.

THIRSTY WORK

Officials hand out drinks of water to the runners 11km into the race and then at every 5km or so after that. Wet sponges are also handed out at regular intervals to help keep the runners cool.

DID YOU KNOW?

The first ever modern Olympic marathon was won by a penniless Greek shepherd in 1896. As well as a gold medal, he was presented with a horse and cart for his village!

Marathon world and Olympic records are regarded as "unofficial" because each marathon course is slightly different.

In the 1988 marathon, 118 runners took part — the largest number of people ever to compete in a single Olympic event!

INDEX

COUNTRY ABBREVIATIONS

AUS – Australia
BUL – Bulgaria
CAN – Canada
CHN – China
DEN – Denmark
ETH – Ethiopia
ECU – Ecuador
FIN – Finland
FRA – France
GBR – Great Britain
GDR – East Germany (1949-90)
GER – Germany
GRE – Greece
ITA – Italy
JAM – Jamaica

KEN – Kenya
KOR – Korea
MAR – Morocco
MEX – Mexico
NED – Netherlands
NOR – Norway
POR – Portugal
QAT – Qatar
GRE – Greece
ROM – Romania

RSA – South Africa
RUS – Russia
SWE – Sweden
TCH – Czechoslovakia (to 1993)
URS – Soviet Union (USSR – 1922-92)
USA – United States of America